# World to World

CAMINO DEL SOL

A Latina and Latino Literary Series

# World to World

VALERIE MARTÍNEZ

The University of Arizona Press

Tucson

The University of Arizona Press
© 2004 Valerie Martínez
First printing
All rights reserved
∞ This book is printed on acid-free, archival-quality paper.
Manufactured in the United States of America
09  08  07  06  05  04    6  5  4  3  2  1

Library of Congress Cataloging-in-Publication Data
Martínez, Valerie.
World to world / Valerie Martínez.
p. cm.—(Camino del sol)
ISBN 0-8165-2375-4 (Paper: alk. paper)
I. Title. II. Series.
PS3563.A73345W67 2004
811'.54—dc22
2003021023

British Library Cataloguing-in-Publication Data
A catalogue record for this book is available from the British Library.

Publication of this book is made possible in part by the proceeds of a permanent endowment
created with the assistance of a Challenge Grant from the National Endowment for the
Humanities, a federal agency.

for Agnes Trujillo
*abuela de las empanaditas*
*abuela chispeante*

# Contents

# Invocation

Out of stone
Out of salt-smell
Out of silence and sepulcher
Out of moon-chasing night
Out of dead-of-the-night
Night buoying them up
They come

Out of the mind
Out of dream
Out of reminiscence
Out of figments
Out of gladness
Out of grief
They come

Girls with their earlobes
Boys with their lower lips
Men ravenous
Women of parched thirst
They come

Mothers and eyelashes
Grandfathers and teeth
Fathers with the backs of the neck
Come

Grandmothers and underarms
Daughters and sons aflame

Infants and tongues
They come

O Memory
How you want to cradle them
Drink from the syllables of their lips
How you want to offer them
Your regrets
Tender as fingertips
How you want to punish them
To save them from the deep
O Memory

O Second Sight
They are issuing from corner turns
They are disappearing
They are half-sight
And near-sight
Are out of touch
And into touch

The dead are watching
(See their pupils growing large)
The dead are sleeping
(How they turn their eyes inside)
The dead are swimming
(For the suns are full of distance)
The dead are humming
(Now they wander in new sounds)

Pull them into you
Tether your sighs to their hair
Float among them tonight

O Weary Travelers
So they come

Ask them to speak in tongues you cannot know
Listen as if the sounds
Are the bones of prophecy
O Dumbfounded Ones

Show them your birthmarks
Your thin lines
Your braille veins
And numb scars
For they have none to trace and lament
Show them

They come in ribboned skirts
They come in linen and earth
They come with nothing to see
They come with everything under the skin

In nakedness
In cloth unwinding
In absence
So they are lovely
So they come

O Cemetery
O Honorary
O Funerary
Night of the Dead
Help them come

The dead are moonstone

The dead are hollow stone
The dead are mist on the bones
In mother-of-pearl

So fear them
And hold them
In the shadow of your ribs
With open palms

Evening of the crossing
Stars of the passing through
Moon-hole beckoning

O Mouth Curve
O Bodies Double
Evening O Evening

Till the worlds converge
On incantation
O Double Life
And Triple Life

The Sumptuous Hunger
Reunion
Hands upon hair upon
Blue limbs incarnate

O Communion
O Tears upon
Sweet Tears Numenate.

DAY OF THE DEAD, 2000

# ONE

## all day all night anointed

# Crucible

It is mine because it belongs to no one, and I cannot have it.

Because it eludes us, flees and flees.

Like the love he cannot, but desires, but is not love.

The snow plummets.

He slides his rocky fists into her sweater

where it is warm. Heady.

You see.

Here are the iced trees illuminate.

A forest of figures poised,

attitudinal. Say "beautiful."

"Look."

No.

It's the opposite. She tells him.

Here I am.

There is no rain. Nothing freezes and shimmers.

Mouth wants none.

This absent

few seconds.

The red, leaf-like parchment explodes in flames.

Sun of the mind.

See.

How.

She cries he is inside her.

Some weather.

Like the woman in the tree

above the water's burgeon, great belly,

who gives birth anyway.

Says what can be done you cannot name.

Here in the poem.

"Look."

The loves, lovers, soldiers

in a blue war lavender.

So.

Make her

make me.

# Four from the Body

◆◆◆

In the morning, there is the gathering of feet. They are like
hexagrams, tarot cards, palms from the other world. In the
winterish houses this is their hour, unveiled. They and the
earth chatter all day. It is why the wicked and the wise ever gaze
at their feet.

◆◆◆

I am numb at the knee. The scar is a deadened patch in olive-
pink. It says *bicycle and asphalt, stone steps, ragged rock.* It is the
final page in a pad of parchment, peeled. Scorched and torn, it is
a mute thing—stories wagging.

◆◆◆

See how the body end-stops at hip and back and right breast?
Take a string and start at the back. Go through the heart to the
front, then stretch across the belly to the pelvis. Make a knot.
At night, tug at each dark mole. Make me sigh. Make me
wrinkle and fold up.

◆◆◆

These are my own bones, called the collar. Upon them sits my
head. They hold it above a mortal torrent. Like two sonorous
reeds they can sing into your ear at my throat. The neck is their
flute, and here is their song from tongue and mouth, transparent.

# Rock and Marrow

Yes, yes, the inside of morning
is cheekbone, elbow, pelvis.
Elsewhere, as the chlorophyll shrinks
earthward, so does the steady rain.
I imagine the center of the planet
hot and not colorful. You see,
it needn't always be vivid and visible.
Lie low in this monochrome
tangle of limbs. I like it
vague and warm at the center
of the densest of things.

# Nude

Is she lying there where light falters
   in rectangles of brown and bone
as maiden? Is she courtesan, sister,
   slave, wife, student? Has she
been paid to recline so, falling asleep
   like a creature in the afternoon sun,
ankle a point of light piercing?
   Is she somehow nothing of these—
new and capacious in sleepy defiance?
   Against history, then, so the eye
now suffers amnesia. She is not
   desire, not mother, not even bits
of negative and positive space, color
   and shadow. No, not animal.
Is she meek? Is she fearsome then?
   Where does the mind's eye wander
in this numb space? Is this her new redolence?
   She does not exist on the side
of any boundary, nor in the definitive,
   nor for the man's eye upon her
nor the woman's field of esteem.
   And while there is all this limiting,
all this blinking out and blanking,
   something enormous fills the landscape,
pure abundance. So it is
   with all we give away at great cost:
paradise rushes toward emptiness.

# Sun

What is broken          opened
    like the sun
    on the sugar cane
a wave of heat over grass huts and children
    with wire cars
    sticks and old tires
is the heart

    Opened
to everything made of      heat
    regret delight passion
    the agony
of someone's          luck
and some          terror

I saw this
it was the story of a man
    who cheated
    then raged upon his wife
the kindness of women
who nursed her health

    It took place
in a          village
the size of some
American houses
a microcosm
    from there to here

             endless

I am learning
    about the           shattering
    the constant unfolding
of this center within us

I had to learn it
    in the summer
    below the equator
understand it has occurred
forever as I         remember

You have broken something
in me

the village of my heart
disintegrates in the heat
    and Father
    with his tentative hands
comes running

    What is        eternal
    what is ever
blooming in the sun
of the          human
          universe

rage and tenderness
rage and tenderness.

BIG BEND, SWAZILAND

# "Doll"

HANS BELLMER

Start with the shadow behind you
because it is safe. It is straight
and square like the chair
which shoves you to the left,
twisted. Your head is severed,
pushed back behind these breasts
blown up, two grotesque bulbs,
crotch a slit bulb, knees bulbs,
belly round bulb huge
with its eye an accusation.
As if the head belongs there,
hair matted, one eye bland and half-
sheathed, lips suffocated
by a chest about to burst.
You swell, you are swollen,
swelling. *Here*, you say,
*here is what you do and I become.*

# Anecdote

Where the metal is is emptiness.
This time I will not fill it.
Gaping, I push down
the dirty lid, and turn it on its side.

The hills do not rise up,
nor the wind, not even
the dusty field. I walk away

like a verb. I am the nothing
of words, drag the earth
beneath me, an unbearable robe.

# The Angels of Reason

Neither the time nor the season
    for the heavens to crash down
upon them lying there, limitless.
    As if no memory—no movement,
no memory—simply love
    has caught them between its teeth.

The mouths which open to sing
    have none, speaking instead
in tongues pink and off-key,
    saying *here* and *darling,*
and witless until these creatures
come forth and pull loose

whatever is between them—
    cotton, smell of earthen moss
parting rib and pelvis,
    making lovers measure
in real time, sense. What
    crashes into flesh

isn't love, is regret tendered,
    the past with its lies
bringing angels, busy with truth
    and minding history.
Nothing frightens them more:
    all this forgiveness—unsavory
mercy, mercy, mercy.

# No Heat Equal

Coming to the fields and the cane leaves burning
I unfold my hands undone
by night and heat
to workers these shadows
figures against the yellow
white hot miles on fire

Looking through fire into night
I know
these fields one by one
burn through the season
leave the sweet cane stalk
the children steal and suck all day

How the ashes float down
for months
onto each promontory
small and large
and each forehead all day all night
anointed

So I cross
the distance
from my house afflicted
burning for sweetness
to the fields aflame
to the fields shorn

And then
for the grass huts etched against light burning
for the places with no light no flame
for the river and river air unwavering
for darkness with no heat equal

all which is not fire

# TWO

## the secret languages

# They Lean and Wander

It is the clouds, not the singularity.
  And not because they rain
or obscure, float or imitate. No.
  More this mortal miracle
of passing through white
  in your window seat,
and they wobble the airplane
  or better yet, don't.
You find they are mist,
  both diaphanous and perforate.
They can show forth water
  which feeds or destroys,
light which strikes the wondrous eye
  or kills it outright.
A female language.
  Here the clouds lean and wander
your steel-sided vessel.
  See how their silver startles
the particular landscape,
  bolt, crack, electric.

# It's Happening

The hurricane's void eye,
pinwheel furiously rolling across.
A weather-man's grinning fascination.
The winds—so many miles per hour,
so many islands per day.
Where it will sweep, stop.
Smash into.

                        the child
                        half formed
                        face blooming
                        eyes and eye
                        a gauzy visage

This many dead.
The rural places inaccessible.
A man wailing in the debris.
These hills of mud sliding,
houses these matchsticks
floating by. The televisions
flashing; your gazes transfixed.

                    see her? still. across
                the diameter of the storm.
                across, across, feet stuck
                in the spin. there alone.

                        Make of it what you will.
                            Disaster rolls
                        from place to place.

No.
Disasters roll. No.
They emanate
from place.
The air delivers them.
Sky and sky.
The indecipherable missives.

the child
for every body
washing by
at the instant
the heart gives it up
o
smoky
breath

Tracking the storm from here

his knowing hand

to here. Cotton ball pinwheel
perfectly symmetrical.
He can explain, grinning.

o weather o
story of earth o
bent by the moon o
man-made currents o
circle
of influence

Tracking it.
The faces of the dead

                                              stops the grinning
superimposed. Cut
to weather maps. Cut
to whorl and the weather-
woman's beringed hand.


                    o circle
                    influence


                                              I'm not saying
                                          it looks like a face,
                                          a profile, an eye.
                                          I'm saying it is.
                                              I'm saying
                                          there's more to this.
                                              I'm saying
                                          it's happening.


                                          What realm is this?
                                          That? What Other?
                                          Whence the child comes?


                    eye and eye
                    the gauzy visage


                              She's saying *it isn't laid end to end.*
                              She's saying *one upon the other.*
                                  And the eye. And the heart
                                  which follows the eye.


                    all the way through

# Fever

Sparrows in the post office, like hell's bats.
Someone's lips over the belly, divining.
Hands at the loom, prophesying.
Cup, cream, lip—transformed by heat,

then last gasp against hot metal, pillow,
and a little one's thighs, infant-marvelous,
and you are feverish, dear droplets, gate:

infinite effort to keep the eyelids
    apart or face the tremor
of darkness. It is gray, then
    the world closes and once gone
the limbs begin to lift
    and it is the slow,
methodical flight of
      dream—

if the image goes. if it goes
    and then we fly.
    and these are words,
and these are words losing
    form    and they
disappear
    and there is    air

and there is earth and air
    under them

# The Eye of Earth

So the stream goes by in ringlets,
and the shine blinks and blinks
and your eyes are there like those
fixed on a flame, like those
in the spell of an ember, calm
and remarkably steady.

Otherwise you might be away
from the forest, or at your desk,
or in the irises of someone
come to cast you away into love,
or in books—all at this moment
utterly misplaced.

The eye of earth is meek right here,
ferocious elsewhere, swallowing
cities with its fiery mouth.
But meek right here, might hurt
as much in some meticulous way.

You are wayward. Now you know.
It isn't contemplation. Not reflection.
No, the mountain has no will
and so it shines and is pure.
You become yourself suddenly.
You are offered up:
rare, stark, enormous.

# Heritage

I hear sounds unlike my own.

Coo of syllables. Coo-cradles.

The red earth moving beneath.

Avalanche of history, with blood.

A mother-house, father-house.

The five plus one, cacophonous.

A girl's deft fingers, ever so.

Polite, *sin* intuit. Belying it.

The man infamous, car dangerous.

Now he has no voice, no cock, no hands.

Marauder. Plunder of marauders.

Adolescent of the wails-cum-words.

Belly-gone-convex-gone-concave.

The crave, crave and starve.

Secret books. The looping black marks.

Where the silence, silence was:

a rocky noise.

# Hollow Where You Are

### I

Past one a.m. Limbs are folding
and unfolding, cool then hot,
azaleas red-dark, awake
on the terrace, in their stony boxes.
I lace my hands, imitate the tangled
synapses of the brain you explain
as I sculpt them of muggy air.
Folding and unfolding. Sweet
midnight. Hip to hip, cell to cell,
stems wound under the unblinkable
stars. This laying on, under, into.
This over, above, beneath, beside.

### II

We are in the boat's belly.
The wind makes it a cradle.
There is this rocking of lips,
one into another. The sea
trembles below as if smitten.
Cracks whistle, rattling latches
chatter as if to startle us:
*O briny lullaby, O wind*
*which snaps the bough,*
*O hollow where you are*
*swaying and swaddled.*

### III

Embedded,
not even the breadth

37

of one of these dragonflies
gathering feverish around our heads.
We're sleepy, unaware.

The autumn sun, the one
that floats upon my knee,
aquamarine and prehistoric,
with the boats in the distance,
tethered umbilical to buoys.
Cloudy iridescence.
A cleaving and cleaving.

IV

The moon beyond frost and window glass.
Flutter of the veiny nest,
nest misshapen, your hand
on my pelvis, ambivalent.
Then the bundle of cells
with our milky tattoos—gone.

I woke, sleep in the membranes,
sedate flush, flash of bluesy
wings I thought I saw, never
to touch, the faintest
breathy flutter, half-heard,
at the edge of the unformed world.

# Fire

So this is my house wavering
        this and this melted or smoking
        that and that burned black
        as if the fire must be
                redundant
        naming and renaming itself

These bodies rushing to and fro
        hands black chalk fingerprints
        these metaphors
                *O Disaster*

One's life opening
                utterly
        silk gown burned through
        books opened ashes
        curling helplessly
        naked before
                strangers
        come upon the house
                mute
                as darkness

Believing
        the letters
        and underthings
        speak their secret        languages
        to me only—no

they are                *desire*

they are                          *whisper*
        to thieves
        to flame
        to bad luck

comes in threes
comes in fives
they are                          *whisper whisper*

through numb fingers
        over sidewalks
        into plastic bags
dragged
through the ax-splintered
doors

they are                          *relinquishing*
                                  languid
        at last
        utterly giving of
themselves

        desire redundant
        these hard and delicate
        objects

once faithful
then flame
now     tatters
        breath
        and black wind

                                  thoroughly
                                  selfless

# World to World

FOR TIM TRUJILLO

1951–1991

I discover the Buddha in the back yard,
    black paint on wood, head tilted,
smile so tranquil. Then the dead come
    over the grass, the garden stones,
a bed of wildflowers, without sound,
    mouths silent as under-earth.
We needn't have any words,
    the dead and I, just holy imagery,
the message *they come*, the secret
    passage under the wall, the creature
who climbs through, the sky
    over the clouds over the air over the earth,
world to world, this afternoon,
    someone I am someone I knew,
the layers beneath the layers.

# Heat of Breath

ANCIENT SEMITES TAUGHT THAT THE SACRUM (SACRED BONE)
AT THE BASE OF THE SPINE CONTAINED A MYSTICAL SEED OF
EACH PERSON'S FUTURE RESURRECTED BODY.
—BARBARA G. WALKER

And so,
  in the end,
the cloud which takes the shape
  of neck, torso, and foot, exhaled
from a mouth in the back,
  is a cloak somehow familiar.
What will the body be there?
  Mirror-Image?  Hush of the Past?
Who planted this seed,
  fed by flesh, speaking its name
from first light to darkness.
  Whose mouth blows into it
with love, loverly, heat
  of breath. And so,
who makes us?

# THREE

## no tear or distance

# Is It the Sun

tender tender as recollection
the sheets unfold a woman
into air

              she questions light
spilling onto a wood floor
reflecting a rose-purple wall

       she asks

*is it the sun which startles memory?*
*is it the light which snaps it closed?*

the doors inside the house become
              doors
                nothing else
and so resist memory

the sun is a red ball of heat
                nothing other

its lingering light could be the past
its light fingering is nothing else

*is it the crush of light that remembers?*
*is it forcing light back to the sun?*

she will give this up
become simply

47

eyelashes and flesh
a bowl of peaches
brown sugar and milk

and so freeing herself
            *sun, sun collapsing*

it comes back to her complete
from some dark and
                  oblivion

# Elegy

Here is the dewy imprint, dip
in yellow cotton, where you lay,
where you. Lay down so
many months ago.
No, years.
Still here?
Weight's ghost.
I try to crush our limbs
into this sunny depression—
femur, rib, breastbone—
hopelessly ceremonial.

# Winter Tableau

Here is the pageantry: flicker
    of some gold, gesture
of the mouth in speech,
    excavation in a valley
where the sun falls gradually
    to a pyramid. It is the altar
of human curiosity, a relief
    against the evening, inked.
This stele, dusty medallion
    some *where*, some distant tableau
against earth, dusk, and sky.
    Here in the poet's mind,
sliced away from all that is
    mundane and tedious;
essential and unreal,
    of air and ink, luminous.

# Bowl

Turn it over and look up
into the sphere of heaven.
The tracery is lucent,
light seeping through to write,
white-ink your face, upturned.

Swing it below
and it's a cradle of blue water,
the sea, a womb.
A mixing bowl
for Babylonian gods.
Here, they whirl up the cosmos.

Pick it up and your hands
form a pedestal,
and all who drink
contain the arcs
of body and the universe—
and between them,

no imaginable tear or distance.

# Odalisque

## I. ROOM OF NUDES

This is how. Here.
Her body. Hers.
And hers.
Wholly or partially
disrobed.

The hair—
black-opaque,
red-brown,
marigold.

Flesh.

Renoir-plenty,
she-pattern-Matisse,
jungle-dark-Rousseau
[her white hands
upright
fearful].
Courbet's gray-pale,
vulvous.

You'll say "Amen."
"Ex-
quisite."
Without
question.

And the "something?"
Inside.
O.

These small and apparent
brushstrokes.

Go further
[inside].
It's nothing.

The nothing
beneath the notion.
That before
the palette.
And before.
The fingers.
Wrist.
His arm with its ragged
cuffed sleeve.
Sinew, nerve,
and synapse.
His stomach,
meager meal,
opiate.

Breath.

Then women, women
swimming
the gray matter.

They
come.

## II. NUDE: RUBENS

All flesh and roundness and thighs
and orange-love and mass these
women as mother-hips.

No.

Girls with almost-breasts
and mother-hips [plenteous].

Synchronous.
Fleshy circumference.

## III. NUDE: VAN GOGH

Horizon-
tal. Public. Pubic.

Shoes and rolled stockings
careless and there
still. *Look*
*at me. Gape.*
*Yes.* Says
Van Gogh
says eyelids says
the body's bold
and cellular
decay.

Watch her.

Unlike his others—
sky roiling
sunflowers
lone peasant
thick-thatched houses.

Her whiteness, weight
descending.

Feel this:
gravitas.

IV. NUDES: SEURAT

Oil.
Point.
Light
unabashed.
Thousands. Tip
of the small brush,
and the wrist's forward
jolt. Again,
again. Again.
He walks backward [see],
forward [jolt]
and back.
And to.
Till the blur
and the ache.
Their nubile.
Vanishing.
Appearing.

Cell. Body. Cell.
Sea of flesh.
Immersed.


V. NUDE: PICASSO

Frontal, profile, level, slant.
Revolve. Turn in space.
Here is the flat surface. Here
the paint makes you
turn, angle, bend.
Wicked corners. Not-curves.
Razors upon razors.
You.
Are.


VI. NUDE: CHRIS TRACY

Woman all one breast and upper arm
and knee-calf twisted compressed
into a box inside a second box
of blue and squared in gold.

No
wonder.

She will. Twist.
Makes her fit.
Makes her.

Fits.

Differently.
Muse. Museum.
[Fruit of the mind's eye.]

This is how. Here.
His body. His.
And his.

Wholly
or partially.

He would recline.
Over and over. Again.
More eyelids than eyes.
Sex passive, hung against
pubis—brown, reddish,
yellow-pale as saffron.
Man-as-father-hips. And.
Their nubile, frontal,
profile, level, slant.
Bellies. All flesh
and roundness.
Wicked corners.
Dabs (jolt).

*watch me. roam*
*as I*
*am.*

[made]

at every turn

VIII. THE ARTIST: SHE

Ex.
quisite?
Her small and apparent
brush strokes.

Make him?
See?

O wonder,
lost, O,
standing, supine,
draped across the blue divan?
Languid?
Vessel?

To make,
make him,
unmake,
make me?

Differently.

Hesi-
tate.

Blank.

# FOUR
## tug of sun

# Flesh and No

AFTER PAINTINGS AND SCULPTURE BY GEORGIA O'KEEFFE

### "GREEN LINES AND PINK" (1919)

These in succession: blue, blue-rose, blue-white;
flat, curve, stripe, curve, cylinder. They extend
and contract, extend—and contract. Again.
The air from there to here: translucent,
a pale drizzle. That is all. It is between.
No and every thing.

### "AUTUMN TREE: THE MAPLE" (1924)

Out at you in some strange swoop.
Black and gray out of stained glass,
out of rust cloud and teeming cotton.
Here and here and here the sky—
cerulean, tiny beyond.
The tentacles' menacing thrust.
Desire. Their relentless grasp.

### "LITTLE HOUSE WITH FLAGPOLE" (1925)

Ring around a neat half-moon. Gargantuan.
Two lines climb and approach, black electric.
The flagpole up up, impossibly bent,
and arrow hung decidedly
over house and clean gray curve.
Little tree illogical, transparent.
Saying *go like we go*—*up, over, along*—
*without the literal, with the no*
*and no of reason.*

## "BLEEDING HEART" (1932)

One upon the other, and inside.
Whereso it is carmine on rouge
on corn-gold on green.
Here the inmost turns on itself.
Pulsate. The weight of what curls up
and comes down, paling. Up
and white-petal-white descending.
If the heart could. How? So.


## "ABSTRACTION, 1945"

Contained within her, air and absence,
the o the arc become back
and arched-up head.
The no of her, moss-black,
not figure at all, abstract
as the body poised, supple,
still. Flesh and no at once.
Flesh and no.
Oblivious.


## "PATIO DOOR WITH GREEN LEAF" (1956)

Cannot but think of the tongue,
the tongue on fire. It floats,
as does the oblique darkness
of door, the wall going left,
a sky's blue mist lifting. Here
is the eye's ruse, suspension,
the leaf gone green and hot yellow.
The breath. The utter silence.
Gone aloft.

## "PINK AND GREEN" (1960)

You are above. No, beside. No.
This swerving pea-green
may not be river,
be snake in the pink fields
or contemplative clouds.
Why make this what it is not:
certain, nameable, distinct.
As if it were not the edge—
cool glance at the other world,
the eye's cataractical brilliance.

# Aureole

The child removes the brass plate,
the harness around her ears.
The play is done. Her part,
scribbles on index cards, scattered
on the wooden, backstage floor.
Round makeup mirrors
with their white bulbs,
halo after halo, blowing out.

Circlet of gold, thousand-petaled
lotus at the head, light rounding
the dark curls of the sage
who rolls her lips and tongue
into the trees.

Despite the sheet, the plastic amulet,
she did feel something surge up
playing Aura of Rome—
through femur, belly, and skull.
Will she know? Whether legend,
earth aspiring, tug of sun—
these magnets of heaven.

# Matter, Hunger, Storm

As if this pale delicacy: petal,
and the fire around it,
and some hint of ash,
and a time lapse,
the brown eye that sees.

As if the gesture: desert,
and the dark skin, women's hands,
and the silk not theirs,
vanishing years,
the clouds' gradual descending.

As if the poor: bending,
and the knees on fire,
and some dull shimmer,
the flash forward
to aching, blue thunder.

As the dust lifts;
as the tender, underneath.
As the ankles.
As the.
As.

A wicked lightning.

# September, 2001

Who scatters the bones, bus stop, sun.
Torso wrapped tight. Trigger button.
How many. Heavy. Much.

You with the dark hair. You
with the conviction. You
with your paradisal maidens.

Come crashing in.
Deliberate.

Surprise.

There is no music no goblets
no table of golden loaves.
If I am virgin, it matters not.
Your eyes are disparate—
knuckles, arms, windows—
blown apart.

Now, find your hands,
and there is one task:
harvest.

This is how the dead work.

BECAUSE you have scattered
flesh, marrow, breath,
writ the bloody writ.

THUS you'll live every specific
agony. Your own. Each one.
Family. Every friend.
It goes on.

NOW gather it.
Make it whole again.

Don't ask how.

Here you go, wandering:
shrapnel, earlobes,
inky red-blue, bits of bone.
Everywhere. Wherever.

What? No light?
(and I am so comely)
Messy? Cold?

What comes together sparks,
makes heat, sumptuous,
whole and blessed,
glows and glows.

# I See, I Am

What dream is this, after thunder,
some yawing, the sound
of steel and concrete twisting.
I've seen buildings flutter.
There is no air here.
What was crushing, unbearable,
now fades into this dark swimming.
Earth is intimate, and human voices
lose their gravelly pitch.
O the indescribable
pelvic-shattering pain
become an oily numb.
Breath is a tissue;
I watch it willow into dark
from this body no longer bone
and sinew and nerve aching.
Watch these tissue-swallows,
a flock toward the honeying sun.
The pool I rise out of,
the whale's mouth.
I see I am nothingness, dense.
O dream, O exquisite
dream of mine, magnanimous.

# Wish

Everything she wants she sees
in the dark coin of this child's eye.

Desire lives in her like the secret
of the statue-goddess, when man
mistakes her for a fetish.

It isn't that she's had nothing
in those hollows: heart and pelvis.

Just that the orphan is asking her
with a look of wanting,
a mother-look, desiderate.

It could happen anywhere
but does so, finally, here

in the sugar fields, among the stalks
where she finds him sucking cane
in the harvest season.

And everything is gathered
for one second, endless.

He calls to her—his eyes go blind
in the sun. And every absent meal,
vicious cane snake, wish for beauty,

wish for beauty's reprieve, enters her
with sweetness and riches and thunder.

# April Ghazal

AFTER A COLLAGE BY MONICA STAHL

Ritual elephant: do these long legs of steel
deliver you? Is the air up there crisp?

These were young black men. Dozens.
These helmets and batons upon them.

You say half my dreams are yours
and I, a guest, float my dead among them.

An arch within an arch, these old stones
carve light into shut-eyed curves.

What we crave predicts abandonment.
How many times must I learn this.

A man and a gun. An angry man's poised
weapon. A madman and suicidal disciples.

See this face? What are the years between
this and death? The skin slackened, luminous.

The cinquain over the couplet's loneliness.
A drizzle over the very married, snow-born ice.

Relentless. You're the ink. Terrible sweetness.
*Lilies of the flesh, lilies of the flesh.*

# Ocean Once Over This

Here they stand, rotund, and undiluted with grief.
Their hands are full of violets, invisible.
The velvet of their garments blows
almost imperceptibly over the ground.
Heaven is a room hemmed by wishes,
recently neglected, near enough to perfume
the skin

here, in the second realm
where paradise lingers,
something on the tongue
we vaguely know.
The garden doing its best
to reach through:
lilac, cherry blossom, cool breeze
ruining the heat.
Wishes slip even as we clutch
and clutch. Even as we grin.

2.

We cannot explain our love of mountains,
clay-red, dotted with piñon, chamisa, yucca.
Perhaps it is the expanse between them,
the sky which fills the space, immense,
the breath opened up like a holy book
blank and ever-blue, on and on

3.

Now the gangs appropriate
the Virgin of Guadalupe.

Needled into their arms.
Screened onto cotton.
Scribbled with boxy, tilted
gang tags for protection.

The pallbearers wear her image
one after the other,
until she blurs under the casket,
the boy with a bullet in his neck.

They feel him passing over.
They choose her because pain
is the passing, reaching through.

They know it.
They know it and know it.

4.

The girl feels her body as nothingness.
Nothingness makes her an angel.
Angels may not be unloved.
Unloved, the body hides itself,
itself—or disappears into air

5.

They surround themselves with creatures terribly injured—
a puppy with four broken legs, crushed by a yellow car.
They fill the tub and work his tiny limbs, numb. He's
forgotten they should move, lies with a stick all day, tail
wagging. Lively half-life.

Who could? Why?
Because he's here?
Because half there?


6.

*under the surface*

the sea

echo & blur of voices
every physical thing

undulating


slowed-down time
blue-green
distant kin

sing


*on the surface*

terror

green veneer
the dark & invisible

beneath

behemoth
impending

enormousness

## 7

The place on the mesa.
The heat and no sleep for two days.
The corn pollen.
The medicine man chanting over her.
The smoke of the pipe in her lungs.
The talisman, feathers, terrible hunger.
The liquid drunk.
It makes her vomit

into the buzzing lack of heat sunset silhouette
the antelope and words so sharp each syllable
is the umbilical thread tugging world to world


8.

It is why the creeping down
is like the bent knees,
crossed legs, forehead
to the ground, hands
pressed together, words
a delirious fever
could be all or one anguish:
devotion, bereft love, deliverance.


9.

I step into the garden (with its hint of bodies)
where the roots spin into trunks and branches,
into yellow blossoms then fruit. Elemental
even as the house upon the ground, hung by air.

The layering. The interpenetration.

I say *hint of bodies.*
I say *ocean once over this.*
I say *every creature before us.*
I say *this world and the others*

reaching
reaching through

# Notes

"Doll" refers to the Hans Bellmer photograph with the same title from the late 1930s.

"No Heat Equal" is indebted to the poetry of A. R. Ammons. "Is It the Sun" and "Anecdote" echo Wallace Stevens.

"They Lean and Wander" is for Sawnie Morris.

"It's Happening" is a response to hurricane Mitch in Central America in 1998, the deadliest Atlantic hurricane since 1780. It claimed more than 11,000 lives.

The epigraph to "Heat of Breath" comes from *The Women's Dictionary of Symbols and Sacred Objects*, copyright © 1988 by Barbara G. Walker; reprinted by permission of HarperCollins Publishers Inc. "Bowl" and "Aureole" were sparked, in part, by the same volume.

"Odalisque" refers to various paintings in the permanent collection of the Barnes Foundation, Merion, Pennsylvania. "Nude: Chris Tracy" (in the same poem) refers to the painter's "Fragment II."

The O'Keeffe paintings and sculpture that inspired "Flesh and No" can be found in the Georgia O'Keeffe Museum in Santa Fe and/or the inaugural catalogue for that collection.

"September, 2001" is a response to the resumption of suicide bombings, in Israel, after a six-week hiatus.

The phrase "lilies of the flesh," in "April Ghazal," is from "Vision," by Uruguay's Delmira Agustini (1886–1914), translated by Valerie Martínez.

# Acknowledgments

My deepest appreciation goes to Amy Pence, Lisa Sewell, and Sawnie Morris whose generous time and attention brought this book to completion. Thanks also to Patti Hartmann and the staff of the University of Arizona Press for their wise counsel.

I would like to acknowledge the following journals and anthologies where these poems (sometimes in earlier versions, with different titles) appeared: *AGNI*: "The Angels of Reason"; *Borderlands: Texas Poetry Review*: "Invocation" and "It's Happening"; *Heliotrope*: "Anecdote" and "Is It the Sun"; *Colorado Review*: "I See, I Am"; *New American Poetry: A Bread Loaf Anthology*: "Ocean Once Over This" (with the title "Ever So, Between"); *New Mexico Culture Net*: "No Heat Equal"; *Notre Dame Review*: "Heritage" and "Hollow Where You Are"; *Renaming Ecstasy: Latino Writings on the Sacred*: "Invocation," "Heat of Breath," and "It's Happening" (with the title "O Story of Influence"); *Touching the Fire: Fifteen Poets of Today's Latino Renaissance*: "Wish" (with the title "Traveler") and "Sun" (with the title "The Human Universe"); *World Order*: "Heat of Breath," "World to World," "Aureole," "The Eye of Earth," "Nude," and "Bowl."

# About the Author

Valerie Martínez's first book of poems, *Absence Luminescent* (1999), won the Larry Levis Prize and a Greenwall Grant from the Academy of American Poets. Her poems have appeared in many anthologies, including *American Poetry: The Next Generation* (2000); *The New American Poets: A Bread Loaf Anthology* (2000); *Touching the Fire: Fifteen Poets of Today's Latino Renaissance* (1998); *The Best American Poetry, 1996,* and *Renaming Ecstasy: Latino Writings on the Sacred* (2003). Her poetry and translations (from the Spanish) have appeared in numerous journals and magazines, including *Parnassus, AGNI, Puerto del Sol, Confluence, Prairie Schooner, LUNA, the Bloomsbury Review,* and the *Colorado Review.* She was assistant editor of the anthology *Reinventing the Enemy's Language: Contemporary Writing by Native Women of North America* (1997), and her selected translations of Uruguay's Delmira Agustini (1886–1914), entitled *Lilies of the Flesh,* is forthcoming. Martinez's essays on poetry and Latino literature have appeared in such literary journals as *Writing on the Edge* and *Tiferet.* She has degrees from Vassar College and the University of Arizona and has traveled widely, including three years in Swaziland, where she taught in rural schools. She has also taught at the University of Arizona, the University of New Mexico, New Mexico Highlands University, and Ursinus College. She is currently Assistant Professor of English and Creative Writing at The College of Santa Fe.